the guide to owning a
Cockatiel

D0795514

Anmarie Barrie

Photo Credits

Glen S. Axelrod: 9 (top)
Joan Balzarini: 25
Rebecca Brega: 59
Jo Cooper: 17
Isabelle Francais: 22 (bottom), 35, 37, 46 (top), 51, 52, 56, 61
Michael Gilroy: 3, 8 (top and bottom), 9 (bottom), 10 (top), 14, 16, 18 (bottom), 23, 26, 32 (top), 55
Eric Ilasenko: 18 (top), 30, 45
Bonnie Jay: 34, 42, 46 (bottom), 60 (top)
Robert Pearcy: 4, 5, 10 (bottom), 11, 28, 49
Rafi Reyes: 1, 57
N. Richmond: 6, 38, 41
John Tyson: 13, 22 (top), 27, 32 (bottom), 36, 39, 40, 43, 44, 47, 58, 60 (bottom), 62

T.F.H. Publications, Inc.
One TFH Plaza
Third and Union Avenues
Neptune City, NJ 07753

This book has been published with the intent to provide accurate and authoritative information in regard to the subject matter within. While every precaution has been taken in preparation of this book, the publisher and author assume no responsibility for errors or omissions. Neither is any liability assumed for damages resulting from the use of the information herein.

ISBN 0-7938-2002-2

www.tfh.com

Contents

Introducing the Cockatiel

Cockatiels are charming, friendly birds that make excellent companions. They are best known for their whistling ability and personable temperaments. In fact, the cockatiel is the second-most popular companion bird in the world and in the US. The cockatiel is easy to tame,

An adult cockatiel is about 11 to 13 inches long and has a very attractive, exotic appearance.

especially if hand-raised by humans, and this bird gets along wonderfully with humans and other bird species alike.

DESCRIPTION OF THE COCKATIEL

Cockatiels belong to the family Cacatuidae of the order Psittaciformes and are classified as *Nymphicus hollandicus.* Adult cockatiels range from 11 to 13 inches (28 to 34 cm) long.

Appearance

Although it is not available in bright colors, the cockatiel is available in numerous attractive variations of white, gray, yellow, and cinnamon. These, together with the orange

The female cockatiel has more gray coloring all over the body and little or no yellow coloring on the head.

cheek patches and yellow crest, make the cockatiel a very attractive, exotic-looking bird.

Cockatiels are dimorphic, meaning there is a visible difference between the male and the female of the species. The general body color of both sexes is gray, slightly darker on the wing feathers and darkest on the long tail feathers.

However, in the male, the outer edges of the wings are white, commencing at the shoulder and forming a band of color down the entire wing. The crest is lemon yellow tipped with gray, and the yellow continues down to cover the forehead, cheeks, and throat. At the outer edges of the yellow, the feathers are suffused with white. The ear patches are orange flecked with yellow. The beak is gray, the eyes brown, and the legs are gray.

The female hen has similar coloring to the male, but the yellow and orange on the head are less extensive. The crest is very pale, sometimes almost gray. The underside of the tail is yellow barred with gray. There may be variable amounts of yellow on the primary flight feathers.

Personality and Temperament

There are numerous qualities that contribute to this bird's growing popularity. The cockatiel has a very pleasant temperament, a temperament that probably cannot be matched by any other bird of comparable size. It is a hardy bird and can be kept with

Cockatiels tame easily, have lively and affectionate personalities, and make great pets overall.

almost any other species of bird, which is rare for parrots of this size.

Cockatiels also make great pets in general. They tame easily and can usually learn to speak a few words. They are excellent whistlers, and they gracefully mimic other birds' songs. However, their own voices are soft and pleasing when compared to the shrill or raucous voices of other birds in the parrot family.

Cockatiels are affectionate birds that develop lively personalities suited to their specific owners, and they are quite content being either the only bird in the house or a member of a flock of companion birds.

Lifespan

Cockatiels have an average lifespan of about 20 years with proper care. Cockatiels do not display their adult coloring until their first molt, which usually occurs between six and nine months of age. Sexual maturity is reached between 6 and 12 months of age.

NATURAL HISTORY

In the wild, cockatiels are found throughout Australia, though not in

In the wild, cockatiels feed on seedling grasses and other vegetation.

the coastal areas. Their natural habitat covers a great area, comparable only to the natural habitat of the Galah cockatoo and the budgerigar (parakeet). They inhabit open or lightly timbered land where they live on seeding grasses and other vegetation that might be available. Usually they are found near watercourses in small groups.

In the northern parts of the continent, they are nomadic and they move from area to area with no set schedule or particular destination. They simply go where the water or food is to be found.

In the south, they are considered to be migratory; their movement is quite seasonal, though many of the birds actually do not follow the rest during the migration. This means that a number of birds remain in an area when most others have flown northward.

Cockatiels prefer to roost on dead or decaying trees, where they also nest without using any nesting material. They have the unusual habit of resting lengthwise on tree barks and branches.

Although they are very peaceful birds, cockatiels are not timid. They are quite capable defending their nests against even the large, long-tailed parakeets found in their native areas. When approached in the wild,

The albino cockatiel is completely white and possesses no color pigment anywhere on his body.

The number of eggs per clutch ranges from four to seven, and they are incubated for 21 to 23 days by both the male and the female. The chicks are fledged after five to six weeks, though the parents continue to feed them for a week or two after this.

COLOR VARIETIES

There are eight color varieties produced in captive-bred cockatiels: albino, lutino, pied, pearled, cinnamon, yellowface, silver, and whiteface. These color varieties mostly describe the pattern of color rather than truly different colors,

The yellow lutino mutation is often mistaken for albino, but there is color pigment present in a lutino cockatiel, even if the color is pale.

they do not panic and fly off. Instead, they merely fly up to the nearest tree (they are ground-feeding birds) to return to carry on feeding the moment the immediate danger is gone. This aspect of their nature is readily seen in an aviary where they merely move along a branch when approached.

Natural Breeding Season

The breeding season for cockatiels in the wild is from August through December in the south, though it may start as early as April in more northern areas. The season is largely determined by the dual availability of rain and seeding grasses.

In the lutino variety (bottom), gray areas are replaced with yellow. Above is a gray pearl male cockatiel.

because in the cockatiel, colors are restricted to gray, white, yellow, and brown on the body and orange cheeks on the face.

You may find many other color combinations advertised than those described here. Some of these are combinations of feather patterns, while others are probably only variants of existing mutations rather than being separate mutations.

Albino

An albino cockatiel possesses no color pigment anywhere on his body,

A cinnamon cockatiel has a brown or tan-colored tone in the gray areas.

so the feathers are completely white. Even the bird's eyes lack melanin and are therefore pink.

Lutino

In the lutino variety, gray areas are replaced with yellow as a result of lost melanin in the feather cells of the gray areas. These birds are sometimes incorrectly identified as white or albino. This is because the intensity of the yellow varies considerably and can be so pale as to appear white.

Pied

The pied is the oldest of the mutations, appearing around 1950 in two different American aviaries. Pieds

The pied is the oldest cockatiel color mutation and is illustrated by patches of white on what would normally be gray areas.

The pearl cockatiel mutation is actually a change in the color pattern, not a change in the color itself.

The whiteface cockatiel lacks any trace of yellow in the mask or body, and there is no orange in the cheek patches.

have irregular patches of white on what are normally gray areas. The amount of white varies greatly; some birds have white covering almost their entire body, while others just have a few small patches.

Pearled

On the pearled cockatiel, small bars of white appear on the wings and body and can extend onto the head. The amount of pearling varies from bird to bird. It was first seen around 1967 in Germany and Belgium. There are many variations of the pearled cockatiel, such as pied pearl, cinnamon pearl, lutino pearl, etc.

Cinnamon

On a cinnamon cockatiel, the melanin is diluted in the gray areas, giving off a brown effect. This can vary from a cream color to a much darker color. The cinnamon variation is known as "Isabella" in mainland Europe and first appeared in the 1960s.

Yellowface

As suggested by the name, the face of this cockatiel is yellow and does not exhibit the orange cheek patches. This is the most recent mutation and is available at considerably high prices and usually only to breeders at this time.

Silver

The gray area of the cockatiel is diluted to appear silver in this mutation. The eye color is usually red. This is a very difficult mutation to come by because it is easy to confuse a light-gray cockatiel with a silver. It first made its appearance in the 1950s.

Whiteface

Whiteface cockatiels have gray on their bodies, but their faces are white. They are one of the latest mutations in which the yellow and orange of the head is lost. Whiteface cockatiels are becoming more popular.

Choosing a Cockatiel

Purchasing a cockatiel as a pet is not as simple as it may first appear. Caring for a cockatiel is a serious responsibility. You must, of course, be committed to the care of any pet, but with a bird as friendly and as intelligent as a cockatiel, that care includes a lot of time beyond just

Cockatiels are intelligent and social creatures that need frequent attention and social interaction.

Make sure you have the time, energy, and finances required for providing a cockatiel with the best care possible.

providing a clean cage, food, and water. Therefore, it is best to be prepared for all of the responsibilities that come with cockatiel ownership and to know what to look for when deciding on the perfect cockatiel for your home and family.

IS THE COCKATIEL RIGHT FOR YOU?

Time Outside of the Cage

Cockatiels are highly intelligent birds and are at their best when they are content and able to move without a lot of restriction. Therefore, it is necessary to provide your cockatiel with a lot of time outside of his cage on an everyday basis.

This does not mean that you have to let your cockatiel fly wildly around your house. Most times, your cockatiel will be content perching on your shoulder, clambering up your leg while you are sitting, or just happily sitting on top of his cage or scampering around his play gym.

You may even opt to trim your cockatiel's wings—this is a bit like a haircut, and it involves trimming down the flight feathers (these will grow back.) This may prevent him from running into any dangers or causing damage to items in your house. Either way, it is absolutely necessary to allow a cockatiel out of the cage every day.

Socialization

All parrots, including cockatiels, are intelligent and social creatures.

Though cockatiels are not difficult to care for, cockatiel ownership is a serious responsibility and should be considered carefully.

In order to maintain your cockatiel's health, he will need a veterinary checkup at least once a year, so be sure to account for this expense.

Therefore, cockatiels need attention and frequent social interaction. This may mean keeping more than one cockatiel or paying a great deal of time and attention to a single cockatiel.

If you get a hand-fed bird and keep him by himself, he will come to bond with you the way he would another bird, and he will want to be your constant companion. Therefore, you must be prepared to spend a lot of time with the bird and provide him with enough stimulation so that he does not get bored. A bored bird may develop bad habits or self-mutilating behaviors, such as plucking his own feathers.

Expenses and Care Requirements

While providing for your cockatiel's emotional and social needs is probably most important, you also need to be prepared for the more basic responsibilities as well. Your cockatiel will need to be fed twice a day, and in order to provide a healthy diet, he will need more than just seeds or pellets—he will need plenty of fruits, vegetables, and other fresh foods as well.

Your cockatiel will need a cage, which will be his home, and all of the other accessories required. Most of these are one-time purchases, however, so you will only have to budget for this expense in the beginning.

You also need to account for the cost of veterinary visits. Even if your cockatiel never becomes sick, you should take him to his avian veterinarian at least once a year for a checkup.

Allergies

If you or anyone in your home has allergies, you should be aware that cockatiels produce powder down, a dusty white substance that triggers allergic symptoms in some people.

Cockatiels and Children

Because they have such friendly temperaments, cockatiels are great companions for children, as long as parents are willing to accept responsibility for the bird's care as well. It's also important to consider whether your child will still be interested in the bird later in life because cockatiels usually live to be at least 20 years old when properly cared for. Will you or someone in your family be willing and able to care for the bird if the child goes to college or cannot have the bird later in life?

If you decide to get a cockatiel for your child, carefully review all of the responsibilities involved with caring for the bird, such as feeding, water, cage cleaning, etc. Also make sure

If you would like a cockatiel that is already hand-tamed, you should obtain one that has been hand-raised by a human caretaker.

If you obtain more than one cockatiel, they will have each other for company when you are not home to spend time with them.

which may be potential threats to a cockatiel? Will you be able to carefully supervise your cockatiel when he is out of the cage? Do you have children or many people living in the house? Would they all be happy with having a cockatiel in the house?

If you have considered all of these things and have decided you have everything required to provide a cockatiel with the proper care and environment, you are now ready to bring a cockatiel into your home!

A healthy bird will have feathers close to the body, clear eyes, and an active, lively demeanor.

the child understands that a cockatiel is a living, breathing creature that requires love, positive attention, and respect. Be clear that the child should not poke or tease the bird or disturb him when he wants to be left alone. It's also a good idea to supervise the child when the bird is out of the cage and to have the child ask for your permission before removing the bird from his cage for any reason.

Will a Cockatiel Fit Into Your Lifestyle?

Another important consideration is whether a pet cockatiel will fit into your lifestyle and your family. Do you have other pets, such as cats or dogs,

You should take your cockatiel to an avian veterinarian within a few days in order to establish your bird's relationship with his vet and to make sure he is healthy.

CHOOSING THE RIGHT COCKATIEL FOR YOU

Age

The best time to get a cockatiel is shortly after he is weaned—meaning that he is eating completely on his own. At this point in his life, a young cockatiel is ready to form lifelong bonds, and you will be getting him while he is eager to learn and free of bad habits. Getting an older bird is just as wonderful, but an older pet may require more time and attention in order for him to bond with you.

Hand-raised or Parent-raised?

A hand-fed baby is one that was taken away from his parents at an early age and reared on formula fed by a human in a syringe or spoon. These birds bond quickly with humans and do not know really know what it is to be "wild." They know nothing except being handled with love and affection by their human caretakers.

It may be a good idea to choose a hand-raised baby cockatiel. They are already hand-tamed, though they are usually more expensive.

Parent-raised birds can be just as great as pets; however, you will have to take the time to hand-tame them yourself.

Male or Female?

Males and females both make

equally good pets, so if you are obtaining only one cockatiel, the sex of your bird is simply a matter of preference. If you are obtaining more than one cockatiel, it's probably best to not get a sexually mature male and female unless you intend to breed them.

How Many?

It is perfectly fine to get a single cockatiel, but he will need more attention and social interaction than a pair or group of cockatiels might require. Owning a single, hand-raised cockatiel requires a substantial time commitment.

If you don't have as much time to commit, buying two hand-raised cockatiels is a solution. This way you will be able to take them out and play with them, but they will have each other at other times.

If you want to house your cockatiel with another bird or even a whole flock, you don't have to restrict yourself to only cockatiels. Cockatiels get along with most other bird species, though some of the larger parrots may be dominating toward a cockatiel.

Finding a Healthy Cockatiel

A healthy bird is lively and active, hopping from perch to perch and making happy vocalizations. The eyes are round and clear, and the nostrils and cere (fleshy area above the beak) are free of discharge. The beak should be well formed and aligned.

Body feathers should lie close to the body and should not have any missing feathers unless the bird is molting. If a recently weaned chick has missing feathers, it may simply be that one of his parents plucked some of the feathers. The feet should have two forward-facing toes and two backward-facing toes all equipped with claws.

If a cockatiel is sleeping on one foot or has a fluffed up appearance, he may be ill. Also make sure the cockatiel has no signs of fecal matter staining the vent. There should be no missing chest feathers either. It's really not a good idea to obtain a sick cockatiel, and you should bring this matter to the attention of the seller.

Once you choose your cockatiel, you should take him to see an avian veterinarian within a few days of your purchase. The veterinarian will be able to ensure that your cockatiel is indeed healthy, and this will also begin the relationship between your cockatiel and his vet. You will need to take your cockatiel to his veterinarian at least once a year for checkups.

Housing Your Cockatiel

Like humans, cockatiels need a safe and secure place to call their home. Therefore, when choosing a cage for your cockatiel, try to select one that will be more than a cage—choose one that will feel like a home.

You can do this by making sure the cage is the proper size, shape, and

When choosing a cage for your cockatiel, try to buy the largest cage you can afford.

The best shape for your cockatiel's cage is square or rectangular.

material and is positioned in an appropriate location. Your cockatiel's cage should be clean, safe, and comfortable. You should also set up the cage before you bring your cockatiel home so that the adjustment period is less stressful for both of you.

THE CAGE

Location

Before you bring home a cage for your cockatiel, you should first decide where in the house you will place the cage. It's important to choose a location that has a lot of activity. If not, your cockatiel will feel lonely and cut off from the family, even if he has another cockatiel to keep him company. You want your cockatiel to feel included and like he is part of the family.

However, you do not want to place the cage in an area that is too noisy or active. Your cockatiel does need time to relax and rest, and he may not feel very safe or secure if there is constant activity going on around him. Living rooms, dens, and family rooms are usually good choices.

You should also make sure to place the cage in a room that has light for

Make sure that the cage you purchase for your cockatiel has horizontal bars—this will make climbing easier.

Select a cage that will feel like a home to your cockatiel. Make sure your companion will have plenty of space and will feel safe.

Cockatiels need perches of many different diameters and shapes to keep their feet healthy. Natural branches, therefore, make excellent perches.

ners—corners make cockatiels feel safe and secure.

At the very least, the cage should be large enough so the bird can fly from one end to the other. It is cruel to confine a bird as active as a cockatiel to a cage so small that he can merely hop from perch to perch.

Make sure the cage you buy has bar spacing that is suited to cockatiels. This means that the bars are close enough together so the bird cannot get his head through the wire. It also means that at least part of the cage will have horizontal bars so that your bird can climb easily. Any doors should latch securely, because cockatiels often figure out how to lift and open unlatched doors.

Cage Material

The best material for your cockatiel's cage is uncoated steel or wrought iron. Plastic on a metal cage is acceptable, but it's best not to buy a cage that has any paint or coating covering it—your cockatiel may chew on this coating, and it can be highly toxic.

Cage Flooring

Your cockatiel's cage should have a slide-out tray at the bottom to make cleaning easy and quick. The best arrangement is to have a wire floor above the tray. In the tray will be some type of nesting material, such as shredded newspaper, which will catch your cockatiel's droppings.

at least some part of the day. Natural light is necessary to your bird's natural schedule. However, don't put the cage in a window or a place with direct sunlight for a long portion of the day because he can get overheated this way.

Size and Shape

How big should the cage be? Buy the largest cage you can afford. You actually don't need to buy a cage that is very tall, but horizontal space is a must.

Therefore, the best shape cage to buy is a large square or rectangle-shaped cage. Round cages are not preferred no matter how large because they don't provide any cor-

CAGE ACCESSORIES

Perches

There are many types of perches available—wood, plastic, braided rope, natural, and even concrete for keeping toenails and beaks trimmed. The important thing is to have perches of different diameters so that the bird's feet get natural exercise. Birds spend much of their time standing, so keeping your cockatiel's feet healthy through varied perches is extremely important.

Place the perches at different heights throughout the cage and take care not to position the perches over any food or water containers.

Toys

Even if you have more than one cockatiel, toys are essential to keep them entertained. Cockatiels are extremely intelligent birds and need constant mental stimulation.

Your pet store will have a large assortment of bird toys that are safe. Avoid toys with loops or holes in which the bird could get his head, wing, or toes caught.

Remember to change the bird's toys often to prevent boredom. This does not mean you have to buy a new toy once a week. Simply rotate them regularly, and the old toys that have been stored for a while will seem "new."

Food and Water Cups

Heavy, round, crock-style dishes are the best choices for serving food and water to your cockatiel. Ceramic and stainless steel are the best materials because they are easy to clean and heavy enough so that your cockatiels cannot easily knock them over. Stay away from plastic because it is not sturdy enough, and also stay away from square or rectangle-shaped dishes—the corners are very difficult to clean thoroughly and can retain bacteria.

No matter how hard you try, a water bowl will usually be dirty with seed hulls, bits of food, pieces of paper, and bird droppings. Therefore, it is necessary to change your bird's water at least once a day. You should also give both the food and water dishes a thorough cleaning at least once a week. It's a good idea to buy two sets of each dish so that you can use one set while the other is being cleaned.

Many cockatiels enjoy rope perches, but you should make sure there are no frayed ends or loops in which his feet can get stuck.

A play gym is an assembly of various toys and obstacles, and your cockatiel will spend countless hours exploring and enjoying this equipment.

Another solution is a water bottle. Every day when you clean the cage, you should tap or squeeze the bottle to make sure a drop comes out, and every few days you must take it off the cage and clean it thoroughly. In fact, having two bottles and rotating them is recommended. Let each dry completely after you clean them. This helps prevent bacteria from growing in them.

Play Gym

A play gym is an assembly of various toys and amusements for your cockatiel, usually fitted to sit on top of the cage. One fitted with a ladder, a network of climbing frames, swinging perches, and toys will give your cockatiel plenty of enjoyment and mental stimulation. Ready-made play gyms can be purchased from most pet stores and come in a variety of shapes, sizes, colors, and price ranges.

COCKATIEL PROOFING YOUR HOME

Because it's necessary to give your cockatiel supervised time outside of his cage every day, you will need to ensure that your house is safe for him. The average room or home actually presents many hazards to a cockatiel, and preventative measures must be taken to make sure your cockatiel will be safe.

Protecting Your Cockatiel from Unsafe Rooms

Some rooms should be off-limits to your cockatiel. One of those rooms is the kitchen. Kitchens have numerous hazards, and most people do not want birds near their food. Furthermore, non-stick cookware is extremely dangerous—even deadly—to birds, and they should be nowhere near any heated non-stick materials. Keep pots on the stove covered, and also cover trashcans and appliances. Make sure there is no water sitting in pots, vases, or a sink that's been left uncovered.

Bathrooms are also potentially dangerous. If you do allow your cockatiel to go into the bathroom, make sure the toilet lid is closed, medicines and cleaners are out of reach, and cabinets and openings are closed off, and also be sure that there is no sitting water accessible to your cockatiel, such as in the bathtub or sink.

Any rooms that have valuable, fragile objects or seriously dangerous objects, such as a fish tank, should also be off-limits to your cockatiel.

Electrical Equipment and Appliances

Cockatiels are great nibblers, so any electrical cords or equipment should be kept away from your bird. If possible, keep the cords and appliances out of reach or tucked away. Check the equipment regularly, and always closely supervise your cockatiel when he is out of his cage.

Make sure any fans, particularly ceiling fans, are turned off when your cockatiel is out of the cage, and also turn off any other appliances that could harm your bird.

Securing Windows and Other Openings

All windows should be kept closed when your cockatiel is out of his cage unless there are strong, secure screens covering the openings—and even then it's probably a good idea to just keep the windows closed. Chimney openings should be covered, along with openings to cabinets, drawers, etc.

Other Pets

Cockatiels can live quite happily alongside cats, dogs, or other pets. However, you should never leave any other pets alone with your cockatiel. Cats are particularly impulsive crea-

tures who react instantly to sudden movements.

OUTDOOR AVIARIES

Another way to house your cockatiel is in an aviary. Aviaries are a great alternative because they allow plenty of flying and exercise space for your cockatiel. They are also the best choice if you would like to house your cockatiel with other birds. Cockatiels can be housed with all types of smaller birds, even the smallest of finches,

Because your cockatiel needs time outside of his cage on a daily basis, you should "cockatiel-proof" your home so that it is safe for him.

providing the aviary is not too small. Cockatiels can sometimes be housed with large birds, but many of the larger species tend to dominate cockatiels.

If you have the time and money to invest in an aviary, the investment will be well worth it. However, if you plan to build an aviary or have one built, make sure you get the appropriate local construction permits. Investigate these permissions in an advance, and draw up suitable construction plans if necessary. It is also a good idea to discuss these ideas with your neighbors if they live close to you and you think the noise may disturb them.

Size and Shape

Like cages, the best overall shape for an aviary is a large square or rectangle. A good size for the aviary is about 10x6 feet (3x1.8 m) with a width of about 6 feet (1.8 m)—this will comfortably house at least two pairs of cockatiels.

Aviary Floor

The best aviary base is concrete or cement, which can be cleaned and hosed down easily. For decoration, you can easily add a layer of gravel over the concrete, which should be hosed down and raked each week.

Dirt is not a sound policy because bird droppings can contaminate the earth. More importantly, mice, rats,

An outdoor aviary is a great housing alternative for cockatiels, especially because they get along so well with other birds.

and other predators can gain access to the birds by burrowing through the dirt. Concrete and cement keep your birds safe from this danger.

AVIARY ACCESSORIES

The Shelter

An aviary should include an enclosed area for your cockatiels to use as a type of bedroom, a place where they will feel comfortable and safe. It may range from simply a roof and sides made of wood to a fully enclosed unit. It can even contain extra storage room where you can store seed and other equipment.

Perches

Perches are necessary for an aviary. These should be placed at each end of the flight area and across the width of the aviary, giving the birds the greatest possible flying area.

Natural branches are preferred and can be made of apple, pear, or other non-toxic fruit tree branches. These natural perches are preferable because they are of varying thickness, which proves better for the cockatiels as it exercises their feet and legs. They are also safe for chewing.

A thick dead branch on one side of the aviary will be appreciated by your cockatiels. However, do not place too many perches in the aviary because they might impede your bird's flight.

Housing your cockatiel in an aviary will allow him plenty of free-flying space as well as exposure to a natural setting.

Bath

A very shallow bathing bowl is a useful addition that your birds will enjoy. One made of concrete is the best. The sides should slope, and one or two small rocks in it will act as stepping stones. Water fountain types look attractive and the birds will use them often, but they will increase the cost of the aviary.

Feeding Your Cockatiel

The area of bird nutrition has undergone massive research, experimentation, and change in the last couple of decades. We now know that an all-seed diet is inadequate for cockatiels and other parrots and that even pellet-based diets need other healthy foods to supplement them.

Fruit and vegetables should be a part of your cockatiel's everyday diet.

Seeds can make up a large portion of your cockatiel's diet as long as they are supplemented with other healthy foods.

Therefore, the key to providing your cockatiel with an adequate diet is variety. Even if you give your cockatiel pellets and a good seed mix, he still needs a wide variety of fruits, vegetables, and other healthy foods in order to receive a balanced diet. The bulk of your cockatiel's diet can be a quality seed mix and/or a specially formulated pellet, but they should be supplemented. A good ratio is 25-percent pellets, 25-percent seeds, and 50-percent fruits, vegetables, and other healthy foods.

PELLETS

Pellets are small, compressed food bits that come in various shapes and sizes, which contain many of the vitamins and nutrients that are necessary for your bird's health.

Pellets can be very colorful, coming in a variety of colors and flavors, while others are plain and uniform in shape and color. Though they are nutritious, some of the nutrients can be lost in processing, and pellets are usually not specifically formulated for the dietary needs of individual species. Pellets are a decent base diet, but they still need to be supplemented with other healthy foods.

SEEDS

Cockatiels do best on seed mixes formulated for parrots. Sunflower seeds are a great treat, but because they are fatty, they should only be fed occasionally and should not make up a bulk of the seed mix. As with pellets, supplement seeds with lots of fruits, vegetables, and other healthy

If you provide a wide variety of foods in your cockatiel's diet, he will be more likely to try new and healthy foods when you offer them.

foods. Cockatiels can easily become interested only in seed, so it is important to introduce your cockatiel to a wide variety of healthy foods from the beginning.

FRUITS AND VEGETABLES

If you base the diet on a seed mix or pellets, you should supplement with fruits and vegetables every day. With a pelleted diet you do not need to be as consistent, though there is no harm in offering these foods on a daily basis. You can feed your bird any fruit or vegetable suitable for human consumption except avocados, which are reported to be toxic to birds.

The key is variety. Feed lots of different foods, taking advantage of what is in season. Especially nutritious are dark-green leafy vegetables and orange vegetables. Raw vegetables

have the most vitamins; they can be chopped or grated, or fed as whole pieces.

Wild plants, such as dandelion, chickweed, plantains, and seeding grasses are also enjoyed by cockatiels.

EGGS

Eggs are a great food for birds. They contain many nutrients, especially the shell, which cockatiels will eat heartily. When feeding the egg with the shell to your cockatiel, make sure to wash the shell thoroughly first, because it can harbor bacteria.

The only drawback to eggs is that they are too rich and fatty to feed every day. Try to feed eggs about once a week. The preferred method is to hard-boil the eggs, then use a sharp

Feeding your cockatiel treats on occasion is perfectly acceptable as long as he receives an otherwise healthy, balanced diet.

knife to slice them lengthwise in half without removing the shell. Remember to remove all fresh foods after a couple of hours so that they will not be eaten after they begin spoiling.

OTHER HEALTHY FOODS

Grains and legumes of all kinds are ideal foods for cockatiels. Brown rice, dry beans, and pasta can be cooked until tender and fed as-is or mixed with vegetables or bread.

Many people bake "birdy bread," which is simply a cornbread recipe with the addition of things such as sunflower seeds and green vegetables. Regular whole-grain breads are also relished by cockatiels and provide a lot of nutrition.

Many cockatiel owners also provide mineral blocks and cuttlebones as treats. The treats are particularly beneficial because they entertain your bird by providing hours of chewing while also providing some valuable minerals.

Remember that the more variety you provide, the better the diet will be, and the more likely your pet will be to try new foods when you offer them.

TREATS

Treats are acceptable on occasion and are great to use as rewards when training.

Sunflower seeds are a real favorite. Your bird will soon let you know what foods he particularly likes. One thing

Fresh, clean water should be available to your cockatiel at all times.

relished by almost all birds is spray millet. This is millet dried in its natural form, still on the stem, and birds go crazy for it.

Never feed your cockatiel caffeine (in coffee, tea, chocolate, or cola) or salt, and an excess of sugar or fat should not be given to your bird either.

WATER

Water should be available for your cockatiel at all times. Individuals vary in the amounts they drink, but all cockatiels need plenty of fresh water. Make sure to change your cockatiel's water container at least once a day, preferably at least twice a day.

Grooming Your Cockatiel

Grooming is very important to your cockatiels, and they will feel their best if they are clean and their feathers are groomed. Fortunately, cockatiels are relatively easy to care for when it comes to grooming, because they will handle most of their grooming needs themselves. The only grooming tasks you'll really have to handle yourself are bathing, nail trimming, and wing clipping (if you prefer to do this).

BATHING

In order to keep their feathers in healthy condition, cockatiels need to bathe. Cockatiels only need to bathe about once a week, but most cockatiels thoroughly enjoy bathing. Therefore, it's a good idea to provide some type of bath for your cockatiel's cage at least once a week.

Most cockatiels look forward to bathing and hold out their feathers with obvious enjoyment. Some may

Cockatiels enjoy grooming themselves and will take care of most of their grooming needs on their own.

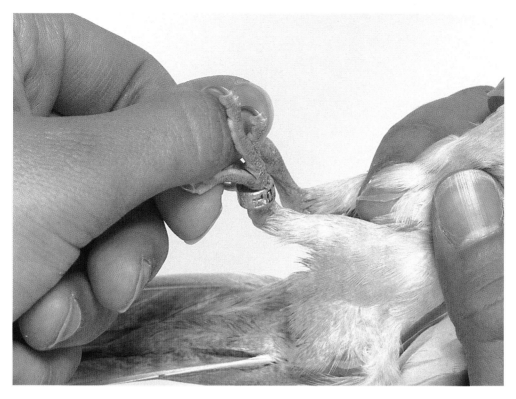

Your cockatiel's toenails should wear down naturally from everyday use, but you will need to trim them yourself if they grow too long.

even enjoy bathing so much that they would choose to do so in your shower! This is fine as long as you keep the shower pressure to a minimum and the water temperature tepid. It is important to make sure that the water is neither too hot nor too cold.

NAIL CLIPPING

If they are not worn down with use, a cockatiel's toenails will grow too long, which will interfere with his ability to get around and could prove dangerous if they get caught and entangled in something. If you do need to trim your cockatiel's nails, you will need several supplies. You should have a towel to wrap your cockatiel in during the trimming process, nail clippers (those made for humans should do fine), and styptic powder, in case the nail is cut too deeply and bleeds. It's also a good idea to have a nail file to smooth the edges after you cut.

You may want to enlist the aid of a helper while clipping your bird's nails. This person can hold your cockatiel gently in a towel while you take on the task of clipping.

When the bird is secure, use a sharp nail clipper to cut the excess nail off. Trim off only the tip of the nail where it is hooked. If you want to use a file, file each nail after you clip it.

The main concern with clipping the nails is that you avoid the quick—the blood vessel deep within the nail. If you should hit the vein, you will not be very deep into it, and a dab with a styptic pencil should stop any bleeding. Remember what the nail looks like at that point, and always trim just a little longer in the future.

WING CLIPPING

Wing clipping is a controversial topic—some people consider it absolutely essential, while others condemn it as mutilation. Those who are in favor of wing clipping feel it keeps the cockatiel safe from escaping or from encountering household dangers. Those who are against wing clipping feel it limits the bird's freedom and robs the cockatiel of his natural flying abilities. The choice is up to you. Keep in mind that wing clipping does not hurt your bird at all, but it does inhibit his natural flying abilities.

Many bird owners trim their bird's wings when they first get him but let

Wing clipping will not hurt your cockatiel if done correctly, but it does inhibit his natural flying abilities.

THE GUIDE TO OWNING A COCKATIEL

If you decide to clip your cockatiel's wings, make sure to have a veterinarian or breeder show you how to do it first.

the feathers grow back with the next molt. By that time he is tamed, trained, and accustomed to his new home. Cockatiels are so affectionate that if your bird was hand-raised, he will probably be so tame and bonded to humans that you will not need to clip his wings to control him.

If you decide to clip the wings, you should have your avian veterinarian or breeder show you how to do this. You may even want to have your cockatiel's veterinarian handle the task every time, but you can do it yourself if you have been taught the correct way by your veterinarian. Wing clipping involves cutting the flight feathers with sharp scissors, straight across. It sounds simple, but you really do need a professional to show you how to do it first. Your cockatiel can be easily injured during wing trimming, so it's important to see how it is done correctly.

You will most likely need a partner to aid you in this task. It's also important that you clip your cockatiel's wings in a very well-lit area. You will need a towel to wrap your cockatiel in, a pair of sharp scissors, styptic powder to stop any bleeding, and needle-nosed pliers (in case you have to pluck a broken blood feather.)

Gather your cockatiel in his towel, and have your partner hold him with one wing spread out. With your scis-

If you trim your cockatiel's wings, you will probably only need to do so a few times a year.

sors, carefully and slowly cut the flight feathers, starting at the wing tips and working inward closer to your cockatiel's body. Cockatiels may need to have several flight feathers cut, though the number you cut depends on the size of your bird's body.

If you trim a blood feather (feathers that have not fully grown in yet), you will have to pluck it out with one quick motion and apply styptic powder to the area immediately to stop the bleeding. If the bleeding does not stop right away, apply some pressure to the area. If it still continues, a trip to the vet will be necessary. This is why it is often a good idea to simply have your veterinarian undertake this task for you.

One solution to the wing clipping controversy is to only clip the wings in the beginning, when your cockatiel is still being tamed. Once he is tame and comfortable in your household, you can allow his wings to grow.

THE GUIDE TO OWNING A COCKATIEL

Your cockatiel's beak will wear down naturally from everyday use, so you should never trim it. If it is overgrowing, this is a problem and you should take him to his avian veterinarian immediately.

Your cockatiel will probably only need his wings clipped a few times a year. You may even decide to clip him in the beginning, while he is still getting used to your family and home, and then allow the wings to grow once he is more mature and adjusted.

IS BEAK TRIMMING NECESSARY?
Your cockatiel's beak should wear down naturally from everyday activities, such as eating, chewing on toys and perches, and picking up objects with his beak. If your cockatiel's beak is not wearing down naturally, there could be a problem. Therefore, you should take him to his avian veterinarian immediately. Never try to trim your cockatiel's beak yourself. Only a professional should handle this task.

Taming and Training

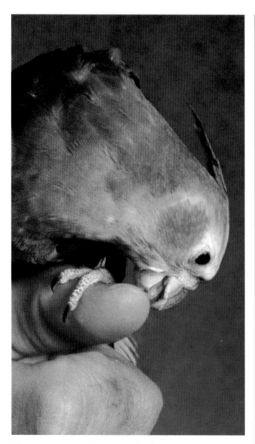

Hand-taming is a gradual process, so it's important to be patient and to allow your cockatiel to come out of the cage on his own time at first.

If your cockatiel was hand-raised rather than parent-raised, he is already hand-tamed and comfortable being handled gently by humans. If he was not hand-raised, rest assured—cockatiels have such a friendly and calm temperament that they are easily hand-tamed.

HAND-TAMING YOUR COCKATIEL

If your cockatiel is not hand-tamed when your purchase him, you will need to hand-tame him yourself if you want to be able to hold him, play with him, or have him come to you after having time outside of his cage. If your cockatiel is young, hand-taming will be fairly easy if you are patient and gentle at all times. It may take longer for older birds, but it will be worth the effort.

Hand-taming should begin when it is quiet and there are no distractions.

At first, your cockatiel may be hesitant to step onto your hand.

The evening is a good time to start taming because cockatiels are usually less active at this time.

How to Hand-Tame

Open the cage door and allow your cockatiel to come out of the cage. It is important to allow your cockatiel to come out of the cage on his own time. If you do have to remove your cockatiel from his cage at some point before he is hand-tamed, drape a small, soft towel over him and remove him—grabbing him with your hands will only frighten him and possibly cause him to lose trust in humans.

Place the cockatiel on the floor of a safe room. It's best to take him to a small room, such as a bathroom, so he will feel secure and won't be able to get himself into any trouble. You can also hold him on your lap in a soft towel if your cockatiel will let you.

Move your hand toward the bird slowly, talking sweetly and gently to him. It is important to be very gradual and patient with this step. If your cockatiel seems frightened or backs

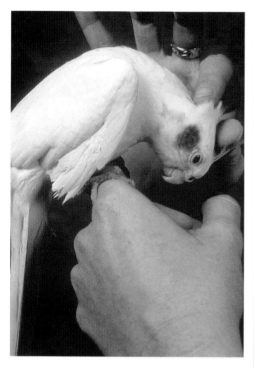

Once your cockatiel is completely hand-tamed and feels comfortable with you, he will probably enjoy being petted or having his head scratched affectionately.

up, do not force the issue. Keep trying to do this until he is comfortable with your hand being near him.

Once he is comfortable and no longer frightened of your hand, move your hand with your palm toward you and your forefinger outstretched toward the bird's stomach. Cockatiels always step upward, so this is why your finger should be directed above the level of your bird's feet.

There is a possibility that your cockatiel may bite your finger, but this is as much to test the solidity of your finger as it is a defensive maneuver. Your cockatiel's bite should not hurt too badly, especially if he is young, so do your best not to respond to the bite at all. You want this to be as positive of an experience as possible, and you don't want him to be afraid of your hand.

Lightly press your finger on your cockatiel's chest. This will force him to step up and onto your finger. Continue to do this, and your cockatiel will soon be stepping onto your finger without hesitation.

Give your cockatiel a favorite treat after each session, and never be in a hurry when taming. Taming becomes easier once the cockatiel realizes he has nothing to fear. Providing that you talk quietly, move slowly, and handle him gently, even adult cockatiels can be tamed. Cockatiels are both bold and inquisitive, and these factors work in your favor. Eventually your cockatiel will perch on your finger and may even let you pet him or massage his head and neck.

TRAINING YOUR COCKATIEL

Once you have hand-tamed your bird and he is always comfortable with you and trusts you, training can begin. Whether you are trying to train your bird to stay off the kitchen counter or to ride a toy scooter, you must use patience and rewards, not discipline. Not all rewards have to be treats—a head scratching and words of praise will also reward your bird for a job well done. Break the desired behavior down into cumulative steps, and work on them one at a time.

You may be surprised to find that as your bird figures out what is going on, he might even anticipate behavior, and he will certainly learn new ones more quickly. By choosing behaviors that are an extension of the bird's natural repertoire, you will make training an enjoyable game for both of you.

Using Positive Reinforcement

When training, it is essential to use positive reinforcement only, which is reinforcing desired behaviors using a positive reward. Rewards can be treats, favorite toys, or praise. *Never* punish your cockatiel. Your cockatiel must be able to trust you in order for training to be effective, and punishment destroys this necessary trust.

Training should always be a positive experience.

Training "Step up" and "Step Down"

Training your cockatiel to step up and step down on command are probably the most valuable lessons you can give your bird. They are important for your cockatiel's safety because you can more easily retrieve him should he escape or get into a dangerous situation. These commands are also good training tools because they serve as foundations for more advanced training. Furthermore, these commands will be handy should you have to move your bird into a travel carrier or remove him from his cage during veterinary trips, cage cleaning, etc.

When training, break down the desired behavior into steps and work on them one at a time.

The step up and step down commands are really just extensions of hand-taming. Once your cockatiel is comfortable being perched on your finger or hand, you will teach him to step onto your hand and off of it at the appropriate times based on the command.

As with hand-taming, lightly press your finger to your bird's chest or belly. This will force him to step up onto your finger. This time, as your bird begins to step onto your finger, say, "Step up." Reward your cockatiel with treats and/or praise and repeat this action, always saying, "Step up" when your bird steps onto your finger or hand. Soon he will do this without much additional encouragement and will respond to the command without you having to press onto his chest or reward him.

Training your cockatiel to step down is very similar. At first, allow your cockatiel to step off of your hand or finger when he wants to. When he does this, say, "Step down" and reward him with a treat or praise. Next, encourage him to step down yourself. Place your hand close to the place where you would like your cockatiel to step onto (such as a perch, the floor, his cage floor, etc.) and say, "Step down." Do not force your cockatiel off of your hand, but encourage him to step off by placing your hand where you want him to go. When he successfully steps off of

Teaching your cockatiel to step up is one of the most important lessons he will learn.

The step up command is particularly useful because you can easily retrieve your companion for trips to the vet, for cage cleaning, or in potentially dangerous situations.

your hand, reward him with treats and praise. As with the step up command, your cockatiel will soon understand that "step down" means that he should step off your hand, and he will eventually do this whenever you tell him to "step down."

Trick Training Your Cockatiel

Although cockatiels aren't renowned for their trick training abilities, most cockatiels can be taught a few tricks. Before you start trick training, pick a quiet room free of distractions where the training will take place. It's also a good idea to only have one person do the trick training, at least in the beginning. Have all supplies ready in this small room where training will be conducted, such as treats and a perch or stand. Also remember to keep training

sessions short. About 10 to 15 minutes is a decent amount of time for a training session, and if your cockatiel seems tired or frustrated sooner than this, there is nothing wrong with shortening the session.

Begin with simple tricks. The easiest tricks for a cockatiel to learn are tricks that are extensions of his normal behavior. A popular trick to teach cockatiels is the wave, where your bird will extend his foot in a waving motion. Your cockatiel should catch onto this fairly easily because it is an extension of his natural behavior to lift his feet.

To teach your cockatiel to wave, have a treat or toy in your hand, hold it just beyond your bird's reach, and say, "Wave." If your cockatiel knows

the step up command well, you can also move your finger toward your bird, but instead of letting him perch on your finger, say, "Wave." Either way, praise or reward your bird for moving his foot, and repeat the process until your bird starts to connect the cue "wave" with the behavior of moving his foot.

Once he has mastered this move, try moving the treat in a wavelike motion, saying, "Wave." Praise or reward your cockatiel when he performs this wavelike motion. Eventually you will be able to eliminate the reward, and he will be able to perform the wave motion just by your verbal cue.

Another simple trick to teach your cockatiel is nodding. Start by holding the treat above your cockatiel's head,

When trick training your cockatiel, begin with tricks that are extensions of normal cockatiel behavior. For instance, walking up a ladder is really just a modified version of step up.

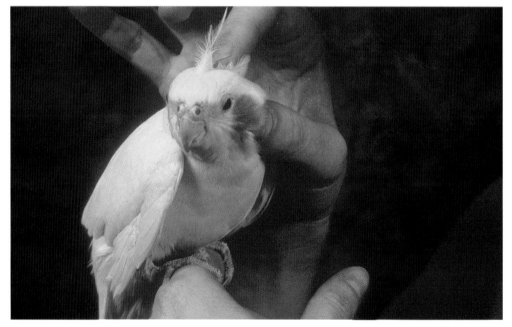

When training your cockatiel, reward him frequently for good behavior with treats or affection and praise.

THE GUIDE TO OWNING A COCKATIEL

keeping it just out of reach. Say, "Nod," and move the treat in a downward motion, bringing it directly in front of his beak and then down past his head, so that his head follows the treat. Give him the treat as a reward and praise him. Repeat this process, using a treat to coax your bird to move his head downward. Once he understands this, use the treat to make him move his head down, back up, and then down again for a complete nod, saying "Nod" as you do so. Repeat this step several times. You may want to move back farther away from him each time if you notice that he is understanding what he is supposed to do when you say, "Nod." Soon you will be able to take away the treat entirely, and he will perform the nod just with your verbal cue.

Some cockatiels may be responsive to more advanced tricks that are popular with parrots, such as basketball or stacking cups. If you decide to train your cockatiel to perform these tricks, remember to break the trick down into very small steps and to praise and reward frequently when

One fairly easy trick to teach your cockatiel is to nod.

your cockatiel correctly performs the steps. Be extremely patient when teaching these more complicated tricks, and if your cockatiel seems to get frustrated, have him perform an easier behavior that he does perform correctly, such as "step up," and reward him for a job well done.

Cockatiel Health Care

The best way to recognize a potential health problem in your cockatiel is to pay close attention to your cockatiel's normal behaviors. You should set aside time each day to study your cockatiel, long enough to notice if he is not looking up to par. Check that he is eating well and generally moving about as normal. If you notice anything out of the ordinary with no obvious cause of the symptoms, you should take your cockatiel to his avian veterinarian right way.

FINDING AN AVIAN VETERINARIAN

Finding an avian veterinarian is absolutely essential as part of the care of your cockatiel. Besides regular checkups, the veterinarian will be available if and when something serious happens to your bird. Many veterinarians are not trained in care for "exotic" animals like the cockatiel and may not be an expert in bird diseases and

Finding an avian veterinarian is one of the most important things you will ever do for your cockatiel.

Paying attention to your cockatiel's normal behaviors is extremely important because you will be more likely to notice a change or problem early on.

treatment. However, avian veterinarians are experts in bird care. Aside from being able to properly diagnose and treat avian ailments, these veterinarians can offer guidance and advice with issues such as training, feeding, and breeding.

You should actually take your cockatiel to his avian veterinarian within the first few days of obtaining him. This way you will be able to develop a relationship with your veterinarian. You should also take your cockatiel for a checkup at least once a year.

If there is a zoo nearby, the veterinarians associated with it may be able to refer you to a colleague in private practice. Regular veterinarians should also be able to recommend a good avian veterinarian in the area, or the store or the breeder from which you obtained your cockatiel can give you a reference.

COMMON COCKATIEL AILMENTS

Only your veterinarian can diagnose and treat any health problems in your cockatiel, so if you suspect that your cockatiel is suffering from some type of ailment or sickness, don't take the risk of diagnosing the problem yourself—take your cockatiel to his avian veterinarian as soon as possible.

Arthritis

Cockatiels who have arthritis will seem uncomfortable when moving certain joints, and moving these joints may seem to take a great deal of effort. Take your cockatiel to the vet right away because there are several ways to make this problem less painful to your bird. Your vet may suggest certain medications, changing the perches, or even changing the bird's diet if he is overweight.

Gout

Gout is actually a form of arthritis and is caused by the accumulation of uric acid due to kidney failure—the kidneys are no longer able to remove nitrogen wastes. Pain and discomfort in the joints are the symptoms of gout. If diagnosed, your veterinarian will most likely prescribe medication and/or changing your cockatiel's diet to help lower the protein level in the diet.

Injuries and Bleeding

Cockatiels are curious, active birds and may get minor scrapes or injuries. Minor bleeding caused by cuts or scrapes usually requires cleaning the area with antiseptic or the use of a styptic pencil. More serious wounds or broken bones require an immediate visit to the vet.

Self-Mutilation

Self-mutilation is a common problem in parrots, including cockatiels. Often this is a behavioral problem triggered by boredom or lack of attention and socialization. If the cockatiel's intelligent mind is not being stimulated enough, he may turn that frustration on himself by plucking his own feathers, picking at his flesh, or picking at his toenails.

Cockatiels are curious, active birds, so take notice in case your bird develops any scrapes or injuries.

If your cockatiel suffers from self-mutilation, try offering him new toys or taking extra time to provide him with love and attention. If the problem still persists, this may signal an actual health problem not related to behavior. Take your cockatiel to his avian veterinarian as soon as possible in this case, because the self-mutilation may indicate a serious medical problem.

Illness and Disease

Only your avian veterinarian should diagnose and treat potential illnesses or diseases. However, you can be aware of some of the symptoms that may signal common illnesses. If you notice that your cockatiel's feathers are fluffed up with his eyes closed, he could be ill. Also look out for watery discharge around the nose and eyes, weight loss, fatigue, or breathing difficulties.

Aspergillosis

Aspergillosis is a fungal disease that commonly affects a cockatiel's lungs. Symptoms are rapid breathing, difficulty breathing, and wheezing. Keeping your bird in clean, well-ventilated areas can help prevent this disease, but if you suspect that your cockatiel is suffering from aspergillosis, make an appointment with your cockatiel's vet.

Polyomavirus

Polyomavirus usually affects young

birds, though adult birds can carry the disease and pass it to their young. Signs of this disease include weakness or fatigue, abnormal feathers, paralysis, and an enlarged abdomen. You should definitely have your veterinarian check your cockatiel (or any birds you have) for this disease. There is no cure or treatment, but there is currently a vaccine.

Psittacosis

Psittacosis is not particularly common, but it is highly contagious and can even be transmitted to humans. The disease is transmitted through droppings and discharge. Cockatiels who suffer from this disease may

The best way to protect your cockatiel from disease and illness is simply to offer him clean, dry, warm living conditions and a healthy, loving environment.

have abnormally colored droppings or show signs of weight loss and fatigue. Humans who suffer from this disease appear to have flu symptoms. There are medications available for both humans and cockatiels who suffer from this disease, so if you suspect either people in your home or birds in your home of suffering from this illness, it's best to take care of it immediately.

Psittacine Beak and Feather Disease

Psittacine Beak and Feather Disease is highly contagious among birds and is often fatal. Symptoms include beak lesions, feather loss, and a weakened condition.

Pacheco's Disease

Pacheco's disease is a highly contagious disease. Strict quarantine is the best preventative measure against this disease. It is a viral infection that affects the liver, and it usually isn't diagnosed until death.

Parasites

The most common parasites of cockatiels are the red mite, the feather mite, and the leg or face mite. Mites are tiny arthropods barely visible to the eye. Some live on the actual host itself, while some live elsewhere but still attack the host.

Red Mite (*Dermanyssus gallinae*)

These mites are usually introduced by new birds, wild birds, or live poultry in the area. They live in crevices of

Many common houseplants or flowers can be poisonous to cockatiels, so it's best to keep any plants out of reach unless you know for certain that they are safe.

woodwork, coming out at night to feed on the blood of their host. When high levels of infestation are reached, the bird scratches and loses sleep.

Old and young birds succumb more easily. They may die from anemia or from secondary infections caused from scratching. Brooding hens may abandon a nest when infestation is high. Feather plucking may commence, which may then become habitual.

Contact your veterinarian immediately if you suspect your bird has these mites. Most likely, cages will need to be sprayed and scrubbed and all nesting material and perches will need to be discarded. If hygiene is as it should be, there is little risk of heavy infestation.

Feather Mite
(*Ornithonyssus sylvirum*)

Feather mites live and reproduce on the host itself. Consequently, they are far easier to control. See your avian veterinarian as soon as possible for treatment.

Scalyface and Leg Mite
(*Knemidocpotes pilae*)

These mites are characterized by horny growths on parts of the face, the upper mandible, and legs. See your avian veterinarian as soon as possible. Treatment in mild cases is by application of liquid paraffin painted on the affected surface. Make regular inspections of the bird after treatment to check for reinfestation.

Household Dangers

Most if not all cleansers, disinfectants, and other household chemicals are poisonous to birds and should not be used around them. Especially dangerous are chemicals designed to kill insects.

Many common houseplants are also toxic, not only to birds but to all animals, including humans. It's best to consider any houseplant poisonous unless you are certain it is not.

Non-stick cookware is also extremely dangerous and potentially deadly. When heated, the non-stick material gives off fumes that are toxic to birds. Never cook using non-stick cookware while your bird is in the room or house. Perhaps even easier is to make sure all of your cookware and appliances are not made from non-stick material.

ISOLATION CAGES

A common cause of spreading infection is the introduction of recently acquired birds immediately into the cage of your original birds. If you have other birds, you should quarantine new birds when you first bring them home. It is not enough simply to put the new bird in another cage; isolation cages are to be as far away from the regular stock as possible. Allow at least ten days to pass for an illness to present itself if possible. If the new bird seems healthy after ten days, you can introduce him to your other birds.

Breeding Cockatiels

Cockatiels are prolific breeders in captivity. Because cockatiels breed so freely, many cockatiel owners choose to breed their pets. However, this is not a decision that should be taken lightly. In fact, most people should *not* breed their cockatiels. Breeding is a serious decision that produces liv-

If you decide to breed your cockatiels, it's best to let a male and female pair naturally.

Breeding pairs should be in excellent health and on a very healthy, nutritious diet.

ing, breathing birds that will need homes and loving care.

THINGS TO CONSIDER BEFORE BREEDING

First and most importantly, you need to consider where the babies will live. Do you have enough space, time, and resources to house them yourself, or do you have other people willing to provide forever homes for all of the babies? If you do not, you should not breed your cockatiel.

Second, you should consider whether you can afford to breed your cockatiel. Many people assume they will make money from breeding, but in actuality, it can be expensive, especially if you plan to hand-feed your babies. Veterinary costs, food and housing expenses, and other supplies can become quite expensive in the long run, so you should be certain that you can afford all of these necessities involved with breeding.

Finally, time is a necessity. If you don't have the time to provide the extra care and attention necessary, you probably should not breed your cockatiels.

If you do, in fact, have the time, money, resources, and potential homes for the babies, and you have carefully made the decision to breed your cockatiel, you can probably have a successful breeding plan if you follow the correct steps and go into breeding fully prepared.

PAIRING AND COMPATIBILITY

Cockatiels have their own ideas as to which member of the opposite sex makes an ideal partner. One male cockatiel and one female cockatiel do not necessarily equal a pair. Therefore, the best way to ensure success is to allow the birds to pair naturally.

However, you can also buy a proven pair, meaning that they have already produced babies with each other. By obtaining a proven pair, you know they are compatible. This depends completely on the honesty of the seller, however. If you decide to go this route, get a guarantee in writing, which any reputable breeder or store will be more than happy to provide.

BREEDING CONDITION

No birds should be expected to reproduce if they are in less than optimum condition. They should be well exercised and neither too fat nor too thin.

Too much fat affects metabolism, vitamin absorption, and other problems that could potentially result in egg binding in the hen. An overweight cock may not be able to fertilize the eggs. Apart from the internal effects of excess weight, he cannot perch correctly when mating.

A bird that is underweight or "going light" could have a protein imbalance, or its body can actually use up its fat reserves and convert needed muscle protein into carbohydrates for normal energy that should already be present.

Birds in either condition are usually incapable of rearing strong, healthy chicks. Modification of the diet is necessary to get the birds fit.

BREEDING AGE

Cockatiels are capable of breeding by nine months of age and sometimes even younger. However, it is unwise

Because they are such social birds, cockatiels can safely be bred in a colony system, though this would require a very large aviary.

to breed chicks at this young of an age. It's best to wait until they are at least one year old or even a little older, when they are fully mature.

BREEDING SEASON

If allowed, cockatiels will breed throughout the year. However, a pair should not be permitted to rear more than three clutches a year; otherwise, the overall stamina and health of the chicks and the parents can be impaired.

The most favored breeding time is spring. The birds have increasing daylight hours and warmer weather in which to care for their young as the season progresses.

The most favored breeding time is in the spring, when there is warm weather and increasing daylight.

Cockatiels in captivity generally produce four to six eggs and hatch and raise three or four of these to fledglings. Sometimes as many as ten eggs can be laid in a single clutch. However, one pair of birds hatching and raising this many chicks is nearly impossible.

HOUSING YOUR BREEDERS

Cage Breeders

A cage for breeding cockatiels does not need to be very different from a regular cage. Because two birds are involved, it should be roomy, and it will require space for attaching a nest box.

With cage breeding, you can monitor progress and change easily. Checking the nest boxes, banding babies, and keeping track of each pair is greatly simplified when there is only one pair per cage.

Colony Breeders

Because they are also very sociable birds, cockatiels can be bred safely in a colony system. This requires a fairly large aviary, however, because you will need separate nest boxes and territories for each breeding pair.

While there may be some minor squabbling, it is rare for serious fighting to break out. Once breeding is underway and the chicks are growing, it is not unusual for older chicks that have already left the nest to help feed their younger siblings still in the nest.

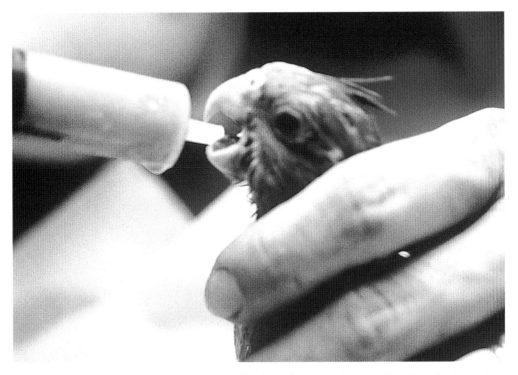

Hand-feeding baby cockatiels is a very difficult and risky task, so enlist the aid of a serious breeder. Never hand-feed without being shown how to do so by a professional.

It is essential that you make sure you have an equal number of males and females, because unpaired birds can cause problems for the nesting pairs. It is even better if you introduce the birds after they have paired.

Nest Boxes

Cockatiels will accept a variety of styles and sizes of nest boxes. The nest box should be placed so that when opened, it is slightly above the level of bedding. It should be large enough to accommodate a pair of cockatiels and between four and eight chicks comfortably.

The access hole should be just large enough for the parents to enter and exit, because cockatiels like secure, protected nesting sites. A wooden ladder should be secured on the internal side of the access hole, and a landing perch should be placed just below the entrance hole.

The material used for the construction of a nest box should be substantially thick to withstand the rigors of wear, an adequate size being about 0.5 inches (1.2 cm) thick. It is also better that the box is screwed together rather than nailed. This way, it can be dismantled and thoroughly cleaned at the end of the breeding period.

Some breeders place a wooden concave shape in the base of the box to prevent the eggs from rolling. You can also simply make a shallow depression in the base and add fresh nesting material every few days.

The incubation period of cockatiel eggs is 21 to 23 days.

The sites for the nest boxes should be sheltered and protected from dampness. Hang nest boxes at the same height (if you have more than one breeding pair), and afford as much space between them as possible. By doing this, you can establish definite territories for each pair.

SPECIAL FEEDING INSTRUCTIONS

Once the chicks hatch, the only food they get is what the parents bring to them, and this ultimately comes from what you feed the parents. The regular daily diet of your cockatiels should already be varied and balanced, but during breeding you should take special care to ensure that the birds receive enough fresh

Cockatiels are unusual among parrots because both the male and female share in the sitting of the eggs.

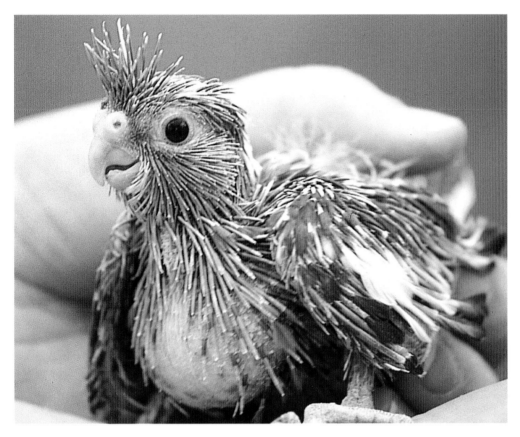
After a baby cockatiel's eyes open at about ten days and the first feathers appear, growth suddenly becomes very rapid.

fruits, vegetables, extra eggs, and soft foods.

Hand-Feeding the Babies

If you wish to learn to hand-feed babies, you should enlist the aid of an experienced breeder. Although an enjoyable task, hand-feeding a large number of baby birds can be quite tedious and nerve-wracking.

Inexperienced owners should *not* undertake this task without a lot of training. The actual process of getting the food into the chick is not difficult to master, but knowing how to spot medical problems before they get too serious is not something you can learn from a few paragraphs in a book. By spending time with an experienced hand-feeder you will pick up the information that you need to raise healthy babies.

INCUBATION

Cockatiels lay their eggs on alternate days and commence incubating after the second or their egg is laid (this will vary from pair to pair). The incubation period is from 21 to 23 days. Ambient temperature will vary the incubation time by a day or two; it takes longer in colder weather than in warmer weather.

Cockatiel chicks fledge at about five to six weeks of age.

REARING AND WEANING

Cockatiels are unusual among parrots because both the male and the female share in the sitting of eggs and the rearing of chicks (a characteristic also practiced by cockatoos).

Shortly after hatching, the chicks are covered with a soft yellow down. (Whiteface and albino chicks are covered in white down.) After about ten days, their eyes open and the first feathers appear. Growth is then rapid. The difference between a chick at three weeks of age and one seven to ten days older is quite amazing.

Normally, chicks will fledge around five to six weeks of age. They continue to be fed by the parents, usually the cock, for another week or two. By this time, the hen has usually started laying a second round of eggs.

Once the chicks leave the nest, watch them to be sure that they are feeding on their own. The chicks can now be socialized and hand-tamed.

Resources

MAGAZINES

Bird Talk
Fancy Publications, Inc.
3 Burroughs
Irvine, CA 92618
Phone: (949) 855-8822
Fax: (949) 855-3045
Website: www.animalnetwork.com/birdtalk

Bird Times
Pet Publishing, Inc.
7-L Dundas Circle
Greensboro, NC 27407
Phone: (336) 292-4047
Fax: (336) 292-4272
E-mail: btsubscription@petpublishing.com
Website: www.birdtimes.com

ORGANIZATIONS

American Federation of Aviculture
P.O. Box 7312
N. Kansas City, MO 64116
Phone: (816) 421-BIRD (2473)
Fax: (816) 421-3214
Website: www.AFAbirds.org

Association of Avian Veterinarians
P.O. Box 811720
Boca Raton, FL 33481
Phone: (561) 393-8901
Fax: (561) 393-8902
Website: www.aav.org

Avicultural Society of America
P.O. Box 5516
Riverside, CA 92517
Website: www.asabirds.org

National Cockatiel Society (NCS)
140 Almy Street
Warwick, RI 02886-3604
E-mail: membership@cockatiels.org or nan-cyr@citilink.net
www.cockatiels.org

North American Cockatiel Society (NACS)
P.O. Box 143
Bethel, CT 06801-0143
E-mail: membership@cockatiel.org or
walkkey@comcast.net
www.cockatiel.org

INTERNET RESOURCES

Avian Network
www.aviannetwork.com

Avian Rescue Online
www.avianrescue.org

Avian Web
www.avianweb.com

The Aviary
www.theaviary.com

Exotic Pet Vet.Net
www.exoticpetvet.net/avian/index.html

World Bird Link Directory
www.aviancompanions.com/links/themeindex.html
Provides an extensive directory of cockatiel-related websites that feature information on general care, breeding, behavior, and health.

RESCUE AND ADOPTION ORGANIZATIONS

The American Society for the Prevention of Cruelty to Animals
424 East 92nd Street
New York, NY 10128-6801
(212) 876-7700
www.aspca.org
E-mail: information@aspca.org

The Humane Society of the United States (HSUS)
2100 L Street, NW
Washington, DC 20037
(202)- 452-1100
www.hsus.org

EMERGENCY SERVICES

Animal Poison Hotline
(888) 232-8870

ASPCA Animal Poison Control Center
(888) 426-4435
www.aspca.org

Index